How to Live
When the Doctors Say You Are
Going to Die

—+—

Doctors don't have the last word!

Joy Haynes

PRESS

www.xulonpress.com

Table of Contents

—✝—

Introduction

—+—

These are the days for people to rise and be healed. There are many books in print today to help the sick and diseased obtain their healing. Then once they've received it, they need to be taught how to keep it! But all too often, we hear of people turning away from God and turning to the world's system for the answer, and they end up dying anyway! Am I saying doctors should not be consulted, and that medicine cannot heal? **Absolutely Not**! I have had to be treated by physicians and take medicine myself on many different occasions...

There is a place in God, a refuge and a strong tower where we can go when disease strikes. Doctors can be involved, hear from heaven and minister the right prescriptions that can aid in our healing! But Jesus Christ, the Divine Physician ministers the Healing Balm of Gilead, which flows from heaven and ministers life and health. When we look to Him, He will lead, direct and guide the physicians with Divine Wisdom, along with the healing anointing that affects health and a cure!

This book is written first of all to glorify the Divine Physician, Jesus Christ the Healer. Secondly, I want to testify of His healing power so that you too can be healed. He has healed me many times in my life, and I want to share these testimonies to inspire you. Our Jesus is no respecter of persons! (Romans 2:11) What He has done for me, He will do for you!

As you read this book, see yourself healed and whole! It will do you good to paint a picture in your Spirit of a strong, vibrant healthy person who is full of life and energy! Go to the banqueting table that He has prepared for us and receive your healing. This book is to exhort you to "Rise and be healed in Jesus Name!

Abundant Love,
JOY*********

CHAPTER ONE

Life Begins at Death's Door

—+—

*And the Lord Said "Indeed Satan has asked for you
that he may sift you as wheat............" Luke 22:31*

THIS IS THE STORY OF MY LIFE!

I was born and raised in a family of nine children. I was
one of two sets of twins born to my parents. At birth I was
not expected to live. However God had other plans for my
life and according to *Jeremiah 29:11*, dying at birth was not
to be my expected end! *"For I know the thoughts that I think
toward you, saith the Lord, thoughts of peace and not of evil,
to give you an expected end" (KJV)*. The Lord does not plan
sickness for you to encounter in your lives. He thinks good
thoughts of us, and health and healing is one of them!

My mother, being a strong determined woman, took my
twin sister and me home from the hospital after birth. We were
both so tiny and weak, that we were put into shoeboxes and
placed in front of a wooden stove where we were kept warm.
The fires of an old fashioned wood burning stove served as

an incubator. As time went by, we grew stronger each day until we could be placed in a tiny crib. We lay side by side, near the crackling fire that burned night and day providing the warmth that our tiny bodies needed, and serving as an incubator at that time. You can imagine the joy it brought to my mother's heart to see her two precious babies, who once were underweight, weak and lethargic, becoming stronger and healthier each day. This brought her hope that all would be well with the both of us.

However, the good health that we experienced during those first months was only for a short time. At six months old, evil darkened our door step. Both my twin sister and I were admitted to a local hospital in West Bend, Wisconsin, where we were diagnosed with pneumonia. For many days I lay in a small crib in intensive care with little hope of surviving the pneumonia. I fought for my life once again. I believe from birth on, Satan has asked for me, that he may sift me as wheat. This seems to have been the story of my life. As the doctors made their morning rounds they gave my mother little hope each time she inquired about my condition, the report was negative day after day. There didn't seem to be a glimmer of hope as my body temperature continued to rise and my lungs filled with fluid and infection. They could only advise her to prepare for my death.

My twin sister was in another hospital room, but was considered not to be as critical. She wasn't in intensive care. My mother told me the story many times as a child. She said I had double pneumonia (which meant it was in both my lungs) and my sister had it in only one lung. Back then, in the 40's, they didn't have the antibiotics that they have today to combat the infection and pneumonia that was a common cause of death. My condition was critical while hers was satisfactory. As time marched on, I continued to struggle between life and death!

Streams of sunlight shone into the nursery, where my mother so gently rocked and held my twin sister close to her breast. I remember Mom telling me when I was a child, about that very day. Every time she told the story it was never without a tear in her eye and a note of sadness and grief in her voice. As she rocked my sister in her arms, she glanced down at her, as it seemed as though her baby girl had become so quiet and still. To her dismay and horror she found her baby was not breathing. As she called for help, it was within seconds she heard the announcement, "Code Blue" and then medical staff rushing into the room. The baby was taken from my mother's arms and all she could do was stand and watch the skilled medical team work quickly and intensely providing all life saving measures. All efforts to revive my twin sister failed and she was pronounced dead within minutes.

Grief and sorrow filled my mother's heart that very moment. The days ahead for Mom were bleak and tearful as she mourned the loss of her child while trying to cope with another one in intensive care also dying according to the doctors daily grim reports. Pneumonia in both lungs, fighting for every breath I took, and high fevers wracked my tiny body throughout the day and into the night hours.

As the days passed, and the funeral was held, to everyone's surprise there came a ray of hope that it seemed as though I was taking a turn for the better. It seemed as the nights turned into days, a renewed strength slowly came to me and I was showing signs of life over death more and more each day. This was a miracle as my mother had recalled the negative reports, but soon those reports began to fade away and a new kind of hope entered the picture.

Within a period of time, I was discharged from the hospital and taken home, where tender loving care was the best medicine for me as I wholly recovered. Incidentally, at the age of 47 after having a chest x-ray, the doctor commented that I must have had a serious condition of pneumonia as a child. He said the scars were still evident even after all those years.

For the second time, (the first time being at birth), Satan desired to have me, but his plans were thwarted, and I lived to the Glory of God.

One might ask "why" my twin sister died and not me? It is important to know that God is Sovereign and knows all things. Deuteronomy 29:29 says, " *The secret things belong to the Lord our God, but those things which are revealed belong to us!*" In this my faith rests alone! We cannot understand the workings of God by rational thinking alone. He has not revealed it to me, so I rest in His sovereign love. I rest in the knowledge I have of Him that He is good, and all good things come from Him, the Father of Lights! We must be firmly rooted in the truths of God, or when deep sufferings and tragedy comes, we will be tempted to make God our adversary instead of our advocate! Sickness and disease are of the devil. Satan will visit household after household if he is not resisted! *He has come to kill, steal and destroy. (John 10:10)* He has stolen children from parents time after time. Why wasn't he able to destroy me? Why did I live when I should have died? Once again..........*the secret things belong to the Lord our God.* They have not been revealed to

CHAPTER TWO

A Visit From Hell!

—+—

I continued to grow as a healthy child. I remember my Sunday School Days. How I anticipated Sundays with exuberance and great excitement. I loved the word of God. I never remember a day in my life that I didn't love God. I loved my Sunday school lessons and would save every one of them. I would read them over and over.

Often I would climb the big oak tree in the back of our house to the highest branch and preach those Sunday school lessons to the wheat and cornfields. I would pretend the stalks of corn were people, and the wheat that swayed back and forth on windy days was the congregation.

I loved to play with dolls. I can remember baptizing every doll that I had. Most young girls enjoyed playing "house" in those days, but, most of all I enjoyed playing church. I would set the dolls in a row, and preach to them as well!

I had a favorite kitten whose name was Twinkle Toes. She was baptized along with the dolls! As a child I thought at that time if there was a kitty heaven I wanted her to go there baptized!

We had a very sturdy homemade wooden swing set out behind the big farmhouse where we lived. Very often I would go out there and swing as high as I could. I always thought someday I might reach heaven if I could swing high enough. As I swung, I would sing ever so loudly "Jesus Loves Me".........whenever I sang "this I know".... there was an assurance that came to me, that He loved me and watched over me night and day.

Two particular times, I remember very clearly going to the swing set to start out my venture towards heaven. Both times, just as I sat on the swing and began to swing, the ground opened up. As I watched the ground breaking before me I began to swing. I was terrified at first, because out of the ground came a huge black bird with no head. His wings began to flap and it seemed as though he was trying to make his way towards me, where I was swinging through the air.

When I began to sing, "Jesus Loves Me" with a boisterous tone of voice, the creature began to sink back into the ground from which it came up. The huge black ugly bird began to sink back into the ground, and the earth returned to its original state. I jumped off the swing set, ran into the house and looked for my Sunday school lessons. Then I began to read them as I had done so many times before! Fear would leave and I would once again rest in the arms of my wonderful Savior.

Ps.27: 1 The Lord is my light and my salvation; Whom shall I fear? The Lord is the strength of my life; of whom shall I be afraid.

I never shared these incidents with anyone, at least not until I was in my late 30's when I had learned of someone else having a similar experience. It was not until then in my life that I had come to the conclusion that it is possible to have a real visit from hell.

I believe that by proclaiming the Name of Jesus in that simple child like song, it backed that creature right up, and back into the ground. Had I not made mention of Jesus Name it is possible that I would have been harmed.

Parents, please teach your children how to use the Name of Jesus. It will be a sure protection to them, should they ever need it.

CHAPTER THREE

More Days Spent In Intensive Care!

———+———

And Jesus said..........Indeed Satan has asked for you that he may sift you as wheat." Luke 22:31

At the age of 10, I suddenly became acutely ill. After being admitted to the same hospital as I mentioned previously in Chapter One, in West Bend, Wisconsin, I was diagnosed with appendicitis. It was a beautiful warm sunny day in March on a late spring, Friday afternoon. The doctors ran blood tests as my mother sat patiently by my bedside awaiting the results. I noticed the worried look on my mother's face as she stared at the doorway. The doctor walked into the room with a grim face and said to my mother, "Your daughter is seriously ill". They made a decision to perform emergency surgery at 7:00 p.m. that evening. My mother walked the hospital corridor several times late that afternoon, ringing her hands and asking me if the pain was getting worse. Nurses hustled around and about my bed, showing concern and yet doing the necessary preparations before surgery. My father came to my bedside after his usual long day at work. During the supper hour I can remember them both looking down at me with long worried faces. Mom and Dad both kept saying, "Now don't be afraid." The best they could they tried to reassure me that everything was going to be alright. Somehow, even at that tender young age I felt as though I was in danger, and it was much more serious than what they were willing to tell me.

I could hear the cart coming down the hallway with its wheels squeaking and clattering. Nurses in their scrub uniforms came in and asked my name. My mother and father quickly verified who I was and as they moved me from the bed to the cart, I remember my mother speaking to me. She was assuring me that all was well and all would be all right. Although there seemed to be a note of concern and worry in her voice, she was making every attempt to keep me as calm as possible. Just like a mother would still the fears of her child, she attempting to do so.

When the doctors began the surgery it didn't take them long to discover something very unusual. They quickly discovered that my appendix were not in there normal place. After much probing and prodding, they eventually found it under my liver. Not only was the appendix in the wrong place, but also to their surprise, it had burst and peritonitis had set in. Another fight for my life had begun. I recall waking up in excruciating unbearable pain and seeing my mother and father standing over me. As a child, I knew something was wrong, because of the extreme pain and the continuous worried looks on my parent's faces. I couldn't speak as I had tubes in my nose and down my throat.

Because the infection was spreading throughout my body, the doctors informed my parents that survival once again was slim. My mother explained to me that I was very sick and that I was in intensive care. At that time I didn't know what "Intensive Care" even meant. But today I believe I was truly in <u>Intensive Care</u>; I was in the hands of my Father who so lovingly watched over me. Many tubes were attached to me, draining the horrible ugly infection from my body around the clock, and once again I fought to live and not die. I was heavily sedated and only woke up intermittently upon being repositioned in bed by the attending nurses. When the nurses aroused me out of the heavy sedated sleep, I recall just wanting to quickly go back to sleep, for that was the only relief of pain I could find.

The day came, however once again when the Doctors were pleased to announce to my parents, they believed I was showing signs of improvement, and they slowly began to disconnect one tube after another. Later I was moved to a private room, where I continued to recover and was sent home with no further complications!

Ps. 91:3-4, " Surely, He shall deliver you from the snare of the fowler and from the noisesome pestilence. He shall cover you with His feathers and under His wings you shall take refuge.

Another round had been won. Another time I was standing at death's door and my life was once again spared. Once again I had been delivered from the snare of the fowler, and even as a child I was thankful for life. Once again another brush with death, but once again another victory in my life. I am so thankful for life to this day. I knew there had been an angelic flurry around and about my bedside night and day keeping watch over me from all harm and danger.

CHAPTER FOUR

A Hannah Heart Cry!

———+———

*And she was in bitterness of soul and wept sore before
the Lord. 1 Samuel 1:10*

*Behold Children are a heritage from the Lord; the
fruit of the womb is a reward. Psalm 127:3*

My greatest desire in life was to Love God with all my
heart, to be a good wife and a loving mother. After
marriage at the age of 18, I found I was unable to conceive
and have children. After five years, when I eventually did
become pregnant, the disappointment was great because a
miscarriage occurred.

Doctor after Doctor informed me it was next to impos-
sible to carry a child full term, let alone conceive, due to
the appendectomy surgery I had as a child. My female
organs were moved around and damaged from that surgery,
thus leaving me unable to bear children. I could not accept
barrenness, as I knew what the scriptures said about bearing
children. I went before the Lord as Hannah did. I cried out to

the Lord from the depths of my heart asking him for a child. Just One! If he would give me one, I would be grateful and not ask again. So I thought!

According to Psalm 113: 9, " He maketh the barren woman to keep house and to be a joyful mother of children."

Praise The Lord! I turned my heart to this scripture and knew that with God all things were possible! With this scripture so alive in my heart, I was determined to bear a child because the word said that He makes the barren woman to keep house and to be a joyful mother of children. So I knew it had to be so.

I went from one gynecologist to another, each one telling me that I would never conceive and that I needed to accept my fate in life.

The day came that I finally conceived and was delighted beyond measure. However my joy was stolen when I miscarried after 8 short weeks of pregnancy. I had two more miscarriages after that, but held on to God, after all He did promise in the scriptures that he makes the barren woman to keep house and to be a joyful mother of children. I was determined he would not leave me childless.

I knew God was still with me as he promised me in the scriptures to never leave me nor forsake me. I had his promise on this.

A short time later my prayers were answered and I once again conceived and nine months later thanked God for the gift of a healthy child. My son was born weighing in at 8 pounds 13 ounces!

My first child brought much delight to my soul. I later returned to the Lord and asked him for another child! My request was granted and I conceived. My second son was born, full term, weighing in at 9 pounds 5 ounces.

Once again, Satan desired to have me and sift me as wheat. The Victory was gained and I no longer was barren but became a joyful mother of children! I also fostered children for five years while my son's were growing up.

Mark 9:23 "...If you can believe, all things are possible to him who believes."

To those of you who might be reading this book and the doctors have told you something similar I encourage you not to receive the evil report. Go to God, and be like Hannah, God is no respecter of persons. What he did for Hannah, me, and thousands of other women He will do for you. Paint a picture in your spirit of giving birth to a healthy child. If you are barren, He will make you a joyful mother. Dare to believe! Dare to take hold of His promises. Dare to step out in faith and say.............I shall no longer be barren, but a joyful mother of a healthy child, or even children if you so desire.

CHAPTER FIVE

Another Walk Through The Valley Of The Shadow Of Death!

—+—

The Life Of The Flesh Is In The Blood.
Leviticus 17:11

The cup of blessings which we bless, is it not the communion of the blood of Christ? The bread in which we break, is it not the Communion of the body of Christ? 1 Corinthians 10:16

It was a beautiful bright cool day in March. I was scheduled for surgery the next day and would check into the hospital that afternoon. The arrangements were made to care for my two children along with two foster girls we were taking care of at the time.

I had been hemorrhaging from my menstrual cycle and the doctors couldn't find the cause. Many attempts with medication were tried, but failed to stop the blood flow that was leaving me anemic. Exploratory surgery was scheduled along with the intentions of performing a hysterectomy.

Before the appointed time to be rolled down to the surgical room, I requested a visit from my home church pastor. I partook of Communion that morning and was confident that Jesus' body was broken so mine could be made whole and that His blood was shed for the remission of my sins. As a partaker of the covenant meal, I knew I was joined together in the body and

Blood of Christ. The Lord's Supper has never simply been a ritual to me. I went to the Communion Table that day with faith, believing all that was provided for me at the cross.

During the surgery I remember waking up. I lifted my head and looked to the side and noticed that bright red blood was flowing through my catheter tube. The doctor said something to me like, " Don't be alarmed, we have called in a pathologist." Then I was injected with another anesthetic and fell into a deep sleep.

Later, upon wakening, I learned that I had kidney failure. It was a puzzle to the doctors. Of course it was another attack to snuff out my life! The doctors were in question as to why this had happened on the operating table. Satan had his plan, and thought this time he might win. The next three days were bleak, as I floated in and out of consciousness. Pain once again wracked my body around the clock, and was evident that I was in for another fight for my life. The Word of God prevailed, and I clung to it as I knew it was my only hope. A kidney biopsy was performed and sent to California. I was given a pint of blood and later recovered without further complications. The biopsy returned negative and there was no explanation medically why the kidney failure occurred! However, I did recover quickly without kidney problems returning a second time! The Angel of the Lord encamped around and about that surgical table and watched over me. I was once again kept alive by the power of the Blood! To God be the Glory for His faithful protection. What Satan meant for evil, my Father, who is greater than all, turned it around for good. Later, I was able to testify of the goodness of the Lord!

The good fight of faith was fought and Satan lost another battle.

CHAPTER SIX

CALLED TO
THE MISSION FIELD

——+——

*Also I heard the voice of the Lord saying," Whom
shall I send and who shall go for us"? Then said I,
"Here I am Lord, Send Me"!*

As the years of my life unfolded, and my children grew
up and went out on their own I found myself in the
Valley of decision!

After 28 years of marriage, my life took a turn. My
marriage was dissolved and I desperately fought the good
fight of faith. I knew I had to go on, as I knew there was a
call of God on my life.

The Lord called me to the mission field. In November
of 1992, I was on a plane headed to Guatemala. I had
committed to a 10-day mission trip, and then planned on
attending Rhema Bible Training Center in Broken Arrow,
OK, the following September. The mission trip proved to be

most fruitful and I was focused on the upcoming direction from the Lord.

The 10-day trip came to a close as we boarded the airplane to return to the states! I awoke that morning not feeling well, but thought it was from something I ate. As the morning lingered on, I became weaker and weaker. By the time I was to board the plane, it was difficult to climb the steps to the aircraft! When I returned home, I was taken to a local hospital emergency room. They ran some tests and told me to return the next day to see my doctor. The next day I went to the doctor's office and he had the results from the tests they ran the day before. He diagnosed me with hepatitis. My liver count was three times above normal and the doctor began admission papers. I was yellow in color and I was in excruciating pain. I asked for some pain medication to get the pain under control so that I could pray and believe God for my healing. He agreed and gave me seventy milligrams of Demerol. I asked to go home and return the next day. He didn't want to agree to that as, he said, I needed to be in the hospital. Finally he did agree that I could come back the next day. He planned on admitting me the next morning. He repeatedly said, "I don't think you understand how seriously ill you really are."

That same morning on the way to the doctor's office, I asked the Holy Spirit what it was that made me so sick. He so graciously told me, it was the Quinine tablets that I took for 14 days during my mission trip. I had a check in my spirit about taking that medication before I took the first tablet, but didn't want to be disobedient. After the doctor diagnosed me with hepatitis, I told him I didn't have hepatitis but it was an allergic reaction to the Quinine tablets. Of course he disagreed but I was so persistent, that he finally went and looked up the allergic reactions to the medication. Sure enough, my symptoms were one of the possible side effects.

I had every symptom of Hepatitis but it was an allergic reaction to the Quinine medication instead.

I returned to my pastor's home where I was living at the time. My dearest friend, Cynthia, my pastor's wife, went out to get me a prescription of pain medication filled. Another dear friend, Joan Merz who is now also pastoring in New Ulm, Minnesota was also with me. She was reading healing scriptures to me. I looked so bad, my friends didn't know if I was going to make it or not. They were quite concerned and prayed diligently for me. I asked Joan to put on some praise and worship music from a particular tape. She put the tape in and I began to worship and praise the Lord. I crawled out of bed and got on my knees and started worshiping the Lord with the music. As I was worshiping Him, healing came to my body. I felt a warm glow from the crown of my head throughout my body! I went down sick but came up well!

The next day when I returned to the doctor healed and whole, he didn't recognize me! Surely he thought I was another person, since the one he saw the day before looked like she was at death's door.

For his own satisfaction, he said I needed to have another liver count to be sure it was normal! The test came back perfectly normal! It is so good to have our Wonderful Holy Spirit tell us all things!

This was an example of another chapter in my life where Satan desires to have me, to sift as wheat! My Pastor later commented that it looked as though he was going to have to bury me! That is how bad I looked and felt! To God be the glory for the things He has done!!! I don't play five inning games, I fight to win and so will you if you want to live long and see good days ahead in your life.

CHAPTER SEVEN

TRIED BY THE FIRE!

—+—

But He knoweth the way that I take. When He has tried me, I shall come forth as Gold.
Job 23:10

O Lord thou art my God; I will exalt thee, I will praise thy name, for thou hast done wonderful things; thy counsels of old are faithfulness and truth.
Isaiah 25:1

In March of 1993, I fully packed my little blue Toyota Tercell and was on my way from Wisconsin to Broken Arrow, Oklahoma. I had enrolled in Rhema Bible Training Center. Since my divorce was final the day I left for Oklahoma, I made a commitment to God that I would not let this destroy me! I would love again and make myself available for remarriage. I knew I wanted to share my life with another, and marry again.

School began in September. In August I met my beloved husband Rick. We were married in October and began our new life together as students at Rhema Bible Training Center!

A few weeks after our marriage, I knew I was entering into menopause and I was having some symptoms, so I went to see a doctor. The doctor suggested I have a mammogram x-ray done for safety measures. To our surprise a breast tumor was found. The radiologist recommended I have a biopsy done immediately. We returned to our regular doctor and the same advice was given.

On the way home from the doctor's office that day, my husband and I were silent as he drove. All kinds of thoughts raced through our heads, but the word of God prevailed. When we got home, my husband immediately cursed that tumor and commanded it to dry up and die in Jesus name. I received my healing by faith right then and there, even though it remained the same size and didn't budge. A few weeks later we were in Stephenville, Texas at my mother-in-law's home. Rick told me if I wanted to have a biopsy done, although we didn't have any insurance, we would get the money somehow as God would provide. He told me the decision was up to me!

I knew, once again, I was being tried by the fire! I took my Bible and went out and sat on the porch swing. It was a beautiful autumn day with blue-sky overhead and the birds singing. I thought about the goodness of God, the love of God, and his mercy! I opened my Bible and began reading. When my eyes came across this scripture I knew it was my answer!

Psalm 35:27 Let them shout for joy and be glad who favor my righteous cause. And let them say continually, let the Lord be magnified who has pleasure in the prosperity of his servants.

God immediately began to speak to my heart through His Word. He was saying to my spirit, He is happy and ever so pleased when we prosper! Prosperity also includes walking in divine health! He said He is thrilled when his own children prosper in wholeness, wellness, health and peace! We are blood bought and He is ever so pleased when we walk in the Covenant of Health! Healthiness, wellness and wholeness were certainly included in the plan of salvation. When I took him as my Lord, I knew I had taken Him as my healer also.

This settled it for me! Now, I am talking about me! A word of caution: If you are going through a similar situation, get alone with God and let Him speak to you as to which avenue you are to take to healing! Don't do it just because Joy Haynes did it. Do whatever He tells you to do. If you have peace about treatment, then follow after peace! I had peace about not going for treatment. Doctor's are your best friend if this is the avenue you are being impressed to take! After all, doctors were given the wisdom and knowledge as how to use medicines.

Months passed! I held fast to this scripture. I repeated this scripture and got it down in my spirit! I went to healing classes at Rhema. They have healing classes for the public to attend in the mornings and afternoons. The dean of Rhema at that time, allowed me to go to healing school in the mornings instead of my regular scheduled classes! I went everyday, twice a day! I went to sleep at night with the Word of God playing continuously on my tape player all night long. It was a tape with nothing but healing scriptures on it. This was medicine to my flesh according to *Pr.4:20-23*. There were also times my husband would sing me to sleep. Every night I went to sleep resting in the arms of my Savior, assured all was well as my husband would so sweetly sing and hold me close in his arms!

35

I wouldn't allow myself to feel the lump in my breast. I was not denying the fact that there was a tumor in my breast. I knew right well it was there, but I was denying its right to exist in my body!

Day after day as I stood in faith on the Holy Written Word of God for healing of this breast tumor, but another attack was launched against my health. It began with symptoms of bone and joint pain. It seemed as though wherever there was a bone in my body and wherever there was a joint, I had pain. It was painful to walk, and to even just move at times. I returned to my family physician once again. After routine tests were run, she so sweetly advised me to consider having a bone scan done. Since my mother had recently died of lung cancer that spread to her bones, and I still had the lump in my breast, she said as nicely as she could, "There may be a suspicion of bone cancer and a bone scan needs to be done." I thanked her kindly and said I would think about it. Once again, I sought the Lord and decided to believe God for my healing.

My husband Rick, once again prayed for me, and we agreed on the Word of God that I would be healed. I continued to attend healing school and sat under the word during classes at Rhema. Also I continued in the Word, as we prayed it throughout the night!

I was doing the laundry one afternoon, as I was praising God I heard the Lord say to me: "Take two aspirin twice a day for one month and you will be healed." Now, I don't mean I heard an audible voice when I say the Lord spoke to me. I heard this in my spirit. I did exactly what I was told to do, without questioning. Within two weeks every symptom had disappeared and I was pain free!

"For as many as are led by the Spirit of God, they are the sons of God." Romans 8:14.

You see, when God has a place in you, when you're tuned into what He has to say, you will be led what to do. Why did He tell me to take two aspirin every day? I don't know, but I obeyed what I heard on the inside, and the pain was relieved and has not returned!

The lump in my breast was discovered in October of 1993. It was now in the spring of the year of 1994. I had returned to the doctor for a scheduled 6-month check-up. After Dr. Susan Willard examined me, with dismay she looked at me and said, "This has grown within six months." She said, she was going to refer me to a surgeon, but would need to schedule me for another mammogram, so he could compare it to the first one. The mammogram was immediately scheduled. It didn't move me though, because I was in full assurance of the Word of God. *1Peter 2:24 By His stripes you are healed.* The word of God was working mightily in me and I wasn't in fear, but at rest in His ever loving arms. *By* his stripes you are healed was my blessed assurance that no matter what it looked like, or what the doctor saw or felt, in the spiritual realm I was healed!

The next day I had an appointment with the Surgeon. To that very day I had not felt the lump; neither did I give it any attention. My heart was fixed trusting in the Word of the Lord! I had purposed in my heart that no matter what, I would not be afraid of evil tidings, but that my gaze would be stayed upon the Lord. Psalm 112:7 was my fortress in my time of trouble again. He shall not be afraid of evil tidings: his heart is fixed, trusting in the Word of the Lord. I want to tell you that I could hear the words of the doctor, who was so loving and kind say to me, "Within the last 6 months the lump has grown." But, I wouldn't allow myself to give those words any attention, neither would I think on them. I gave them no thought, but thought about Psalm 112:7 and 1 Peter 2:24.

My husband and I arrived at the Surgeon's office for the scheduled appointment early the next morning. The Surgeon came in and cheerfully introduced himself. He examined the report of the mammogram carefully, and then examined me. With a rather puzzled look on his face he said, "I can't find anything, and the mammogram also doesn't show anything!"

Now this lump in my breast was present just a few days before, when my family physician examined me. From the reports of the last mammogram, she measured the lump and knew it had grown considerably. I also had the x-rays of the first mammogram taken, with me. The doctor examined the x-ray closely and compared it to the perfect one taken the day before.

The Surgeon appeared to be a bit irritated. He said there isn't anything there. I said, "Praise the Lord, God healed me!" He didn't look very pleased, but I knew there definitely was a divine intervention! The surgeon quickly dismissed himself and left the room. My husband and I rejoiced over the faithfulness and goodness of God, and the truth of the Word, that in another time of crisis it didn't fail us!

It took over 6 months of standing on the Word of God before I was healed. Healing comes to all those whose heart is fixed, and trust in the Word of the Lord!

When you are standing on the Word of God for your healing, you have to look to the author and finisher of your faith. You cannot look at the symptoms. The symptoms will overtake you if you lose focus.

Looking unto Jesus, the author and finisher of our faith... Hebrews 12:2

Even though all hell breaks loose all around and about you, one must steady himself upon the Word. You can only do this by following the commands in

Proverbs 4:20 – 22. My son attend to my words; incline thine ear unto my sayings. Let them not depart from thine eyes; keep them in the midst of thine heart. For they are life unto those that find them, and health to all their flesh.

My heart is fixed trusting in the Word of the Lord! This must be your confession! Turning your eyes upon Jesus, look fully into his wonderful face; this will cause you to look away from the pain
and the symptoms. This is what establishes your heart and keeps you fixed on trusting in the Lord! Remember the Creator of your youth!

Remember the one who knit you and formed you together in your mother's womb! He knows all about your body, and He knows how to heal and repair and restore it back to health, when it has been struck by evil. Sickness and disease are evil and they come from the devil. Don't ever let anyone tell you any different!

When we are being tried by the Fire, let us not forget to exalt Him, and praise His name! For He has done wonderful things! What wonderful things has He done?

Himself took our infirmities and bare our sicknesses. Matthew 8:17

HEALED AND WHOLE! Though Satan desired to have me, and desired to sift me as wheat...the Greater One in me prevailed and led me into healing and health another time! What He has done for me he will do for you! Bless His Holy Name! He takes pleasure.........He wants us well! No parent takes pleasure in seeing his or her child sick with pain. Neither does our Father take pleasure in seeing us in pain...but takes pleasure in seeing us prosper in health and wholeness!!!!!

CHAPTER EIGHT

CALL ON
THE DIVINE PHYSICIAN

—+—

When Jesus heard that, HE SAID: This sickness is not unto death, but for the Glory of God, that the Son of God might be glorified through it.
John 11:4.

My son, give attention to my words; incline your ear unto my sayings. Let them not depart from your eyes, keep them in the midst of your heart. For they are life unto all those that find them and health to all their flesh. Proverbs 4:20 – 22.

I was so blessed to be able to go on a Missions trip with Living Waters in 1992. I went to Guatemala for ten days. We did medical clinics, prayed for the sick, and saw numerous salvations. We were active in street witnessing, and participated in praying for the sick during the evening tent meetings that were held. At the end of the trip, I knew I had been called to the Missions Field, but I also had a witness in my spirit that Guatemala wasn't the place, although I loved the people there and found the trip to be most rewarding and fruitful.

It wasn't until after Rick and I graduated from Bible School, that we had answered the call of God on our lives to go to the Mission Field! After we were married and entered Bible School, we sought the Lord through prayer and had a witness that we were to serve the Lord in China. With great excitement and enthusiasm we boarded a plane to China just two and a half months after graduation.

We served the Lord diligently in this communistic country. As of the writing of this book, we are still serving God there. We were in China about four years, when once again sickness reared its ugly head and the accuser of the brethren paid a visit to this temple of God. Only this time, the attack was launched at my mind!

It all began when I noticed my memory becoming dull and faint at times. By that I mean that the most normal routine things of everyday life were hard to remember. Short term memory seemed to increase rapidly.

We returned to the States to itinerate. One day I was driving down a very familiar street, when I suddenly became aware that I didn't know where I was! This lasted for a few minutes and then I regained my recollection. It was alarming to me at first, but I dismissed it and didn't give it any attention. I thought at times that I was working too hard, and needed to take a few days of rest, and then I would be fine.
A few weeks later, it happened again. I was driving my car down a street, when I realized I was going down the street the wrong way. I had driven this street hundreds of times before without any problems, but this time I was driving against traffic and wasn't aware of what I was doing. In a few moments, I was aware of what was happening but didn't remember how I got there. Thank God I didn't have an

accident injuring other parties. The memory lapses were no longer occasional, but seemed to becoming on a consistent basis.

Our Lives Continued On The Field Despite The Attacks

Rick and I returned to China after being home a few months in the States. The episodes seem to be repeated without any warning. I was teaching an English class in a nearby Government building one day and as I was returning home from the class, I lost conscious of my whereabouts. It was the same familiar street I had taken every day to the building where I taught classes, but didn't know where I was. As the days followed, I began to lose my balance and for no reason whatsoever, I began to fall down while walking.

Another time I was walking home from teaching and fell down on the concrete. I lay there for a moment, not even knowing how to get up. Finally it came to me to pick myself up, but once I was on my feet I was not certain as to where I was, how did I get there, and what had happened to me. With skinned knees and elbows it seemed as though I was in a fog, trying to find my way out. Slowly clarity returned with memory recollection. I just stood there on the sidewalk thinking, what on earth is happening to me?

Many times I would pray in the Spirit and trust the Lord to get me to class. I would teach the class without problems. I had to solely trust the Holy Spirit to help me teach. There were times I wouldn't remember how I even got to school, but when I began to teach there would be a grace that would enable me to teach. Often after class the students commented on the quality of teaching and said I was the best teacher they ever had! I knew this had to be the help of the Holy Spirit, as in myself I was helpless.

Seek The Lord First, Before You Seek The Doctors

My condition seemed to grow worse as the days lingered on. There were more and more occurrences and very often someone would be talking to me and I could hear them, but couldn't understand or comprehend what they were saying. It was the most terrible feeling. I knew something was wrong with my mind. I would often have to stand against this intruder of sickness and disease. I prayed, confessed the word, and held fast to what I knew even on my worst days.

Rick and I decided to go to a hospital in Dalian and have an MRI done. We wanted to see what we might be up against, and to find out the specifics and direction on how to pray.

The morning of the MRI, before we left for the hospital we prayed. We asked for clarification, Wisdom and Knowledge as to what the problem might be. When Rick prayed, I agreed and when we said AMEN, immediately this scripture rose up out of my spirit.

Jesus said: "This sickness is not unto death but for the glory of God, that the Son of God might be glorified thereby". Jn.11: 4

After receiving the results of the MRI, the doctors informed us that there were some arteries that appeared to have some blockage, but nothing serious though. They prescribed a vitamin and sent me on my way.

In the following days to come, the symptoms grew worse and I was losing my balance more often. I couldn't remember things, and I would find myself wondering aimlessly around not knowing which direction to go. Sometimes I would just be outside our apartment. I found myself staring aimlessly into space, and then wondered if I was having mini seizures. Often someone would be talking to me, but I would have this

44

blank look on my face as I was trying to figure out what they were saying to me.

We then decided that I would return to the States with the MRI and ask a neurologist to examine the x-ray, and seek another opinion.

He Will Never neither Leave Me Nor Forsake Me!

Flight arrangements were made for me to leave China. Although Rick wasn't going home with me, I knew I wasn't going alone. I rested in the scripture according to **Hebrews 13:5 "I will never leave thee nor forsake thee!"** Of course, Rick wanted to come with me but I insisted I would be fine and I wanted him to continue teaching my English classes. I wanted to fulfill my contract at the school, although Rick reluctantly agreed to let me travel alone. Rick's family was informed of my scheduled flight home. His sister lovingly agreed to pick me up at the Dallas Fort Worth airport.

Rick wrote all of the instructions and directions out for me as to what to do when checking in, where to go when changing planes, and all else that was involved with traveling internationally. Now, normally I would know what to do since I had done this so many times by myself before. But since the condition of my mental state changed so rapidly we could not trust it. There was never a warning as to when I would suffer from memory loss, thereby not knowing where I was or what I would be doing at the time. I kissed my beloved husband good-bye and boarded the plane. Once again, I had an assurance that all would be well because Jesus said,

"This sickness is not meant unto death but to the glory of God that the Son of God might be glorified"!

45

The flight from China to the U.S. is considerably a long one. Air travel is approximately 19 -20 hours long. This doesn't include the layovers in Beijing, Korea, and San Francisco. The flight however is longest from Seoul, Korea to San Francisco, traveling at an altitude of approximately 35 - 40,000 feet for 12 hours. This is where it seemed as though I became weak. When the plane landed in San Francisco, I felt weak in my body and very faint.

Everyone had to get off the plane for about two hours and then re-board to continue on to Dallas/Ft. Worth. When I got off the plane, I wasn't sure where I was. I only knew I felt exhausted at the time, and followed the crowd to the transition lounge.

During the two-hour layover, I fell into a deep sleep. The next thing I knew, a lounge attendant was calling my name to inform me it was time to get back on the plane. I was confused as to where I might be going, but did as she said and once again, only knew to follow the crowd. Upon take off, I fell back asleep. The next thing I knew the plane was landing in Dallas/Fort Worth.

When I awoke, I knew that my sister in law would be meeting me at the airport, but not sure of anything else. When the plane came to a stop and the seat belt light was turned off, I stood up to walk off the plane. I was seated at the door and recall being the first one off the plane. As I stepped off the plane and into the walkway, I fainted. The next thing I knew, I was in a wheel chair being wheeled down the hallway and over to the baggage area, where my baggage was already waiting. The flight attendants wheeled me quickly through customs and out to the entryway where my sister-in-law (Susie) was waiting. She approached me and began talking to me but I didn't recognize her As we approached her I kept thinking to myself, I wonder where Susie is, why isn't she here? She took me to her van and then had to help me get in. My memory came back as she talked with me.

Because of the weakened condition I was in, she decided to take me to Parkland Hospital in Dallas. Upon arrival there, I was admitted to the neurology floor. After being examined by many doctors, I was asked a series of questions. Most questions I couldn't answer. Simple questions such as the date, my age, the name of our president, etc. I did know my name, which I was grateful for.

I recall another patient being admitted and in critical condition. I remember praying for his salvation. He overdosed on drugs and was badly beaten by another drug user. Although my mind wasn't clear and I seemed to be in a fog, my spirit was alive and soaring. That is why I could pray and believe for the recovery of another person.

A Series Of Tests Begins

A spinal tap was amongst a series of neurological tests that were scheduled for me the following day. The head doctor who was supervising the spinal tap told me she was a born again spirit filled Christian. I was so thankful to have her attending my bedside as the spinal tap was performed. An intern was doing the tap, when he slipped with the needle and hit the spine. This sent my body into tremors causing me to go into shock. I felt like I had been electrocuted. This not only happened once, but three times. After the second time, the head doctor said she had to be relieved and stepped out of the room while another attending physician took over the procedure. After the procedure was finished I was shaking violently and weeping uncontrollably. The Intern bent down and said, "Joy, you are crying because you are frightened"! I knew he had slipped with the needle, and through my tears and shaking I told him, "There is no fear in me.... you made a mistake." He immediately left the room. Friends were outside my hospital room and each time the needle slip occurred I let out a blood-curdling scream. I had never in my life experienced so much pain.

The spinal tap error left me with excruciating pain down my left leg. I heard the attending Physician instruct the nurse to give me a morphine pain injection. My friends had returned to the room and were amazed to see the kind of condition the spinal tap had left me in. Immediately they began to pray and rebuke the pain. They read scripture to me, which eventually brought relief to where the pain was tolerable.

How wonderful it is to have your own company at your bedside when your life is being threatened! Sometimes you are in a state of pain where you can't pray for yourself! This is why we need one another in the body of Christ. To this day, I am so thankful for their attendance.

My Wife Shall Live and Not Die!

When I was admitted to the hospital, Rick's family e-mailed him in China and told him I was hospitalized. Immediately he e-mailed our office staff in Broken Arrow, Oklahoma and our close and dear friends in Texas. They rushed to my bedside upon hearing the news. Mary, my sister and best friend, immediately flew from Wisconsin to Parkland Hospital. What a comfort it was to have them all there.

Later that afternoon one of our friends, who was at my bedside, told me he would email Rick and inform him of my condition and tell him to come immediately. But the Spirit of God rose up on the inside of me, and even as weak as I was I said "NO! He is not coming home to me sick...I am going home to him well!" I knew this came from down within my Spirit, as I believe it was the Holy Spirit speaking these words through me!

As soon as the report came to Rick that I was hospitalized he began to walk the floor endlessly quoting scripture...all the while believing and confessing, "My wife shall live and not die" along with other scriptures that promised healing and long life! Even though my husband and I were a half of a world apart we were close in heart. There were many times he would continuously turn to his wedding band and recall the love that was so strong between us as he prayed fervently for the recovery of his wife. As I lay in the hospital bed, I would turn my gold wedding band over and over, knowing we were one in spirit, joint heirs of the grace, and that our newly married life was still fresh and I could not leave this earth, as we still had dreams to dream and visions to fulfill. Rick has always told me that I was the wind beneath his wings and I wasn't about to give up that place. I knew he needed me, and I needed him and that a three-cord strand cannot be easily broken. So it was Jesus, Rick and I together, and we would go forth and finish our course. None of this checking out early! Besides who in heaven needs hands laid on them, who in heaven needs deliverance, who in heaven needs to be saved? I would then purpose in my heart, that I was going to be here for the long haul. When I was satisfied with life, then I would call my children and grandchildren to my bedside, pray a blessing over them, pull my knees up to my chest, lay my head back on my pillow, wave good bye and walk right on into eternity with my Savior.

The rest of the day passed by with the pain lingering in my leg. It was so painful that often it would bring tears to my eyes. Nevertheless with encouraging phone calls from pastor friends, my home pastor and his wife in Wisconsin, plus the friends and family at my bedside, I was able to hold fast to what I knew! Many times I would recall what I had always told myself. "Never let your mountain see you cry." It was tough at the time, and though I did give momentarily, I was able to regain control over my feelings and the pain, and press on. An old time favorite scripture of mine is

Philippians 3:14, I press toward the mark for the prize of the high calling of God in Christ Jesus.

It was time to press in, and not give up. I knew I was down, but I also knew that I would rise again! This was no time to quit, give in, shrink back, or draw back. But it was a time in my life to keep pressing on toward the mark for the prize! Many times I had seen the goodness of God, but I knew there was still more. We must never give up. Mountains will come and mountains will go, but never give into your mountain. Speak to it as it says to do so in

Mark 11:23 For verily I say unto you, whosoever shall say unto this mountain, Be thou removed, and be thou cast into the sea; and shall not doubt in his heart, but shall believe that those things which he saith shall come to pass' he shall have whatsoever he saith.

So, I never want my mountain to see my cry. I want it to know that it isn't going to take me under, because I am going over as it is cast into the sea! I am victorious in Christ Jesus, so I have a legal right to go over things, and not be thrust under them!

Death Sentence Pronounced

By the next evening the tests were completed, and the results were all obtained. The pain still was present in my leg, being controlled with pain pills and injections. It was about 6:00 p.m. when two of the assigned doctors to my case walked in the room and stood at the foot of the bed. I was still weak and hadn't been able to walk without falling.

The doctor's voice was soft and gentle as he began to report the results of the tests. With a serious look on his face and a very sympathetic look on the other doctor's face he said, "Even though you are only 52 years old, we don't know the reason or the cause, but your diagnosis is Alzheimer/Dementia. You have the brain of a seventy-five year old woman with this disease. Your brain is like a flower that has shriveled up and is smaller than normal. We are sorry, but you are already in the last stages of Alzheimer's disease and there is nothing Medical Science can do to help you, neither is there any medication you can take to slow down this process. You can return to China to be with your husband, of course with someone accompanying you. Within a short time, perhaps a few months or so, you will not know your name, recognize anyone, or know your whereabouts. More than likely you will die an early death. We seldom see this in a person of your age, as a matter of fact it is rare, but unfortunately it does happen."

The Word of God Was Hid In My Heart

Once again, the Spirit of God rose up within me. I propped myself up on my elbows as I was too weak to sit up, and I heard myself say "OH GOODY"! "BUT YOU DON'T KNOW MY GOD." "YOU DON'T KNOW MY JESUS, MY DIVINE PHYSICIAN"! "YOU DON'T KNOW THAT HE WILL HEAL ME"!

The two doctors looked at me, smiled and said, "Your mind is not right, it isn't functioning right. We have given you our report and can only go by what our findings are and you have Alzheimer's/Dementia." The doctor continued on, in his low soft, but gentle, kind voice. He said that the staff from physical therapy would be coming in to see me. Since I was unable to walk without falling, Physical Therapy would judge my gait. They would observe my walking as they fastened a gait belt around my waist and walked the corridor with me. They determined whether I would need a walker, a cane, or perhaps I possibly even needed a wheel chair. However, the doctor was determined I would need a walking device to aid me in my walking, as he mentioned that it was too dangerous to be stumbling and falling down. He was concerned about me breaking bones on top of everything else!

Before the doctors left the room, they made a special note to tell me that I would need to make an appointment to return to the hospital for another MRI. They planned to shoot a special dye up through my brain. They were going to test the oxygen flow to the brain and perhaps they would be able to increase the flow by medication, which wouldn't buy me any time, but hopefully it would help me retain short memory periods. They didn't seem very hopeful but were willing to try anything! I promised I would make the appointment and return for the test two weeks after my discharge.

I had a choice to make, to choose life or to choose death. I chose life and immediately recalled what Jesus said when we had prayed before going to the hospital to have the MRI that day in our apartment in China. Jesus said,

"This sickness is not meant unto death, but for the glory of God that the Son of God might be glorified thereby".

I am so glad I knew what "Jesus said". Had I not known what Jesus said, my heart would not have been fixed trusting in the Word of the Lord! Whose report do you believe? I believe the report of the Lord! I believed what Jesus said, so I could not accept the evil tidings! Why???? Because "Jesus Said!" And he had a lot more to say about healing than they did, so I hung onto the promises that I knew were for us!

Despite the evil report I was not afraid of bad tidings because my heart was fixed trusting in the Word of the Lord! We are to take heed to what we hear in our spirit, and I could only hear what Jesus said! I heard the doctors' report but I couldn't accept it. You see, sickness knocked on my door and faith answered it with what Jesus said! It was a fact. The doctor's have a responsibility to present you with the facts. We don't deny the facts, but we do deny them the right to exist in our bodies. You see, I knew the truth. I knew that by the stripes of Jesus I was healed. Jesus bore my sickness and carried my pain that I need not carry it. That was truth, and when the truth becomes embedded in your heart, then truth supersedes facts. Know the truth and it will set you free. Set you free of what? Of sickness and disease.

As the days followed and well meaning friends and family would say, "The doctor said"...I could only answer with "But Jesus said"...What did Jesus say? He said,

"This sickness is not meant unto death, but for the Glory of God that the Son of God might be glorified thereby!" (John 11:4)

Physical Therapy Pays A Visit

I glanced at the big round clock on the wall as the Doctor's left the room. It seemed as though my life was wrapped up in that big old red minute hand that went round and round on the clock! At that time it seemed as though the red hand was racing. I recall saying as I starred at the clock, "My times are in your hands, Lord"! I knew time was ticking and I didn't have a lot of it from the doctor's point of view! As I looked away from the clock, two more professionals dressed in long starched white coats approached my bedside. They were two very kind young people, a man and woman. They politely introduced themselves as being from The Physical Therapy Department. They were there to test my gait. They brought with them a walker and explained to me we would walk together down the hall.

They fastened the gait belt tightly around my waist and helped me out of bed and to my feet! The room began to go in another direction. My legs felt like two rubber poles as I glanced down at them whispering, WORK! They didn't obey and I began to fall to the side. With a therapist on either side, one would gently push me back to the middle, but that didn't last as I took another step, I swayed like a drunken man to the other side. They immediately helped me back into bed and said I would need to leave the hospital with the walker they had brought in with them. They instructed me ever so kindly, not to make any attempts trying to walk on my own. I needed the walker and another person assisting me whenever walking to prevent falling and injury to myself!

My spirit being alive unto God began to rise up. I looked up at the attendants as they sweetly pulled the covers over me, looking at me in an apologetic fashion. As they turned to leave the room, I spoke up as loud as I could, pointed to the walker and said "Get that thing out of here!" With amazed looks upon their faces, they both just stood there looking back at me. I repeated it again, "Get that thing out of here"! This time they returned to

the bed, one patting my leg saying, "Now Joy, you cannot walk without it. You must be reasonable!" Her words were full of sympathy, although kind. At that very moment the word of God arose in my heart. According to

Proverbs 24:10, *If thou faint in the day of adversity thy strength is small.*

I knew right then and there it was no time for fainting, no time to rely on my own strength, but to look to the Strength of the Lord!

I was glad when the therapists immediately picked up the walker and left the room. Now let me clarify something here. This is what was in my spirit to do. Not to accept the aide of the walker. For someone else, they may have been led to go another route and take the walking device. That would have been right to do so too. You have to be led by the Spirit of God. I knew that if I left the hospital with that walker, my flesh would want to rely more heavily on it than I would the aide of the Holy Spirit. It would have been easier to accept the walking device, but to say "NO" to it was going to make me concentrate on what I believed.

I threw the covers back, slid to the edge of the bed and lowered myself to the floor. I crawled into the bathroom and pulled myself up to the sink mirror. I looked at myself in the mirror and said, "Legs you be strong and you will walk!" I gave myself a good talking to and knew the fight of faith was on

but I also knew that it would be a good fight! I had the assurance that I had the Victory, even though I would have to fight the fight of faith and hold fast to what I knew! I was the Victor and not the Victim. I crawled back into bed just as the nurse entered the room. She began to scold me for getting out of bed without help. I didn't hear much of what she was saying because I was concentrating on what Jesus said!

"This sickness is not meant unto death, but for the Glory of God, that the Son of God might be glorified thereby!

Discharged From The Hospital

The nurse informed me that I would be discharged that evening as soon as the discharge papers were completed. My sister and sister-in-law entered the room. The nurse asked them to help me get dressed. I told them I could dress myself. They left the room with the nurse reluctantly. When they returned I was fully dressed. It took faith to get to the closet that seemed miles away, to get my clothes, but by the enabling grace of God I sat fully dressed upon their return with the nurse.

My family was crying by this time and so was the nurse. I brightly announced they didn't have to cry for me, as I was going to return for that MRI healed and whole. I would definitely have a new brain upon my return and the x-ray would prove it. The Nurse looked at me puzzled, but said I was glowing as I spoke. I knew it was God because I had my hair slicked back from previous brain wave tests, and had no makeup on. I told her it was the Lord and neither Mary Kay, Max Factor, nor Maybelline could take any credit for it. I also shared with her what Jesus said!

Bleak Days Ahead

I was discharged from the hospital with pain medication for the pain that still shot up and down my left leg. Rick's sister took me to her home. The days ahead were difficult. It was painful for relatives to watch me make attempts to walk and fall. They would jump up quickly and offer their assistance, but I graciously refused it. I commanded my muscles to be strong. I couldn't go by how I felt or what I saw. I could only go by what Jesus said . I couldn't go by how I felt or what I saw. I could only go by what Jesus said!
My family was full of sympathy. They loved me dearly and it hurt their hearts to see me suffer in such a way. The only problem with sympathy is that it never gets anyone healed. As much as they loved me and tried to help me out of the love and goodness of their hearts, had I stayed with them, they would have buried me. They didn't have an understanding at that time of divine healing.

Rick made arrangements from China to have our office staff in Broken Arrow, Oklahoma drive down to Texas to get me. Rick knew the importance of getting me with our own company. I had to surround myself with people of strong faith, who believed that God's Word was medicine to my flesh!

I was taken to a friend's home that cared for me daily. I spent most of my days lying on my bed with healing scriptures plugged in my ears. I slept with the word once again playing night and day. I confessed daily that my

mind was quick, smart sharp, sound and alert with supernatural instant memory recall!

Many times I would go to speak, but lose thought of what I was going to say. Friends and family would want to help me finish my incomplete sentences. I would stop them! I would make the confession and tell my mind to work. This was so difficult, but yet so necessary. My spirit was in charge and it wouldn't let my mind get away with not working right! Thoughts would bombard my mind at times, but I refused to take those thoughts! I answered those thoughts with "But Jesus Said!" I clung to what Jesus said every time someone reminded me about what the doctors said! Every time Satan reminded me what the doctor's report was, I reminded him of what Jesus said. When I quoted what Jesus said, Satan would flee, but nevertheless would return with more reports and thoughts. It was written upon the tables of my heart what JESUS SAID! I believed and therefore spoke night and day what the Word said about healing and what JESUS SAID!!!! His words were medicine to all my flesh! Remember the doctor said there was no medicine that could cure this disease! *Let God be true and all men a liar!* There was medicine available - they just didn't know it!

Revival In The Land! I Want To Go Too!!!!!!!

I was so thankful for my friends' hospitality and care that they gave me! They stood with me along with pastors, staff, and other friends. Thank God for faithful phone calls, cards, letters, and a husband who wouldn't give his wife over to the portals of death.

Late one winter afternoon in February, my friends who were visiting me were sitting on my bed. They were talking about going up to Smithton, Missouri where they heard about a church that was having a revival. The more they talked about it, the more my spirit man began to stir! Finally I said, "I want to go too." They looked at me a bit surprised, but agreed to take me with them. Two days later we were headed for Missouri to attend the Smithton Revival. I knew right well that there was something for me there and that I would never be the same again. I was very weak, but as my friends helped me into the auditorium that evening, I knew I was in the right place.

To my surprise, I found myself gripping the sides of my chair with both hands and saying to my dear friend, "I have come for a miracle and I am not leaving without it. No matter how long it takes I am not leaving without it. You might have to return to Tulsa without me, but I am not leaving here until I get what I came for, and that is a Miracle".

Miracles Are For Today, They Have Not Passed Away as Some Might Say!

The Praise and Worship team came to the platform and before I knew it, I was in the Holy of Holies! I was in the presence of God, as awesome praise and worship leaders led us there! All too suddenly though, the music stopped and I heard Pastor Steve Gray say, "I don't usually do this, matter of fact I don't know if I have ever done this, but as I was standing here worshipping the Lord, I heard the Lord say "Someone has come tonight for a Miracle! Someone is here in need of a Miracle!"

My heart leaped with joy! It's me! It's me! I am the one! "That is me," I proclaimed as I made my way through the crowd. I was sitting in the middle of a long row and had to get to the aisle to go forward for the Miracle I had come for. When I got to the middle of the aisle, I suddenly didn't know where I was. I looked around and thought, who are all these people and why are they all standing here. Where am I and what am I doing here? Thank God for ushers. To this day I respect the calling on an usher. An usher immediately took me by the arm and ushered me to the front. The pastor and his wife stepped off the platform and came to me at once. They never touched me, but held their hands above and around my head and commanded strongholds to be loosed. I fell hard to the floor. I fell under the power of God. I went down one way and came up another. I went down with a diseased brain that was shriveled up like a flower and looked to be that of a 75 year old woman who was in her last stages of Alzheimer's. (This is what the doctors told my family and me that my brain looked like from the x-rays and tests.) I came up healed and whole. I was taken to the platform afterwards and I testified that the power of God surged through my body, leaving my mind clear which had been so clouded for months and days prior. As I testified, I began to preach and fell under the power of God a second time! The power of God was charging throughout my body and I couldn't get up. I tried, but it seemed as though I was glued to the floor. I lay there in the presence of God and let Him sweep through my body and spirit once again making the necessary repairs and correction. Taking out old parts and replacing them with new ones. I knew that I knew on the inside, after I was able to get up off the floor, that I was healed and whole. After I was escorted back to my seat I sat in amazement, thanksgiving, and praise of what the Lord had done for me! I will never forget that day. I went for a miracle, expecting to receive a miracle, and I left with a miracle. A miracle that brought peace to my soul, and energized my spirit.

Another MRI Scheduled

I knew I received the Miracle I requested. I was so thankful. I returned to Tulsa and then went by bus back to Dallas. I was scheduled for another MRI. I was excited for the day to come so that I could go to the doctor's office and report, LOOK WHAT THE LORD HAS DONE. Incidentally, not everyone was as excited about the healing miracle I had received as I was. Some believed it, and some didn't. Those that did, were of our "own company!" They believed in Miracles. They believed in Signs and Wonders! This wasn't anything unusual to them! Others commented that it could be this or that, anything but God! Oh but I knew in my heart what had taken place. Others stood by and waited for another episode of the past to take place. They thought this might just be temporary as they still clung to the doctor's report. After all, the x-ray showed my brain had shrunk up like a flower! I had the brain of a 75-year-old woman in the last stages of Alzheimer's! That was the report they believed, but I believed the report of the Lord. They believed what the doctors said and I believed what Jesus said,

> *"This sickness is not unto death, but for the glory of God that the Son of God might be glorified thereby."*

Satan Goes To Doctors' Offices

It was a crisp winter February Monday afternoon with streams of sunlight shining through the corridors of the doctor's office. I was ushered to a medical room shortly after checking-in. Today was the day the doctor would read the x-ray results to me. I had told everyone what the results were before I even got there. I knew I had a new brain and I also knew the MRI would confirm it! I knew it would be proof to the skeptics who were still waiting for another episode to return and rear its ugly head.

The doctor, with a suspicious look on her face, slowly opened the door, peeked her head in, and said she would be right back. She returned after a few minutes, with a very stern matter-of-fact look upon her face. She immediately began to shoot the exact same questions at me, that were asked over and over the night I was admitted to the hospital! Who is the President? What day is this? What year is this? I am going to give you three words and in 2 minutes I will ask you what they are. To her surprise, I remembered the questions that were asked that night upon admittance. Not only did I remember the questions, but also had all the answers! She looked shocked. She then asked me to draw a clock and place the hands at 11:00. Again, she was surprised as I did it instantly. I was asked to do this several times the night I was admitted to the hospital, but couldn't think how to place the hands to display 11:00. By now her eyebrows were raised. I told her about the pain that remained shooting up and down in my left leg. At times it was so painful that I couldn't sit. I would have to stand or walk around to get relief. I lived on constant doses of Ibuprophen, Extra Strength Tylenol and aspirin. She snapped at me and said it was nothing and I needed not worry about it.

I could feel the tension rising in the room between the two of us. I then asked her for the x-ray results. She said they were not complete. I said I didn't believe it since it had been two weeks or more. Radiology told me the day I had the MRI done, that you would have the results in two or three days. She said, "I can't give you the results." I asked why. She said, "Because they are inconclusive."

Holy Ghost Boldness

Holy Ghost Boldness seemed to come all over me right then and there! I stood to my feet and asked her firmly to please get the results immediately, and if she could not obtain them, I would report to the clinic supervisor that she was withholding information from me that was on my personal chart. She left the room in an angry fashion. About 15 minutes later she returned and said she had the results. I read the radiology report she handed me. The radiology report read: There are no findings of abnormality. The brain is found to be normal and perfect in every way. Praise the Lord! I closed the chart and laid it on the counter. I said, "I have received a miracle from God. He gave me a new brain." She mockingly laughed and made the statement that she didn't believe in miracles. She got in my face and said, "I believe you made this whole thing up and you are making up the pain in your leg as well to get more pain pills! You are unhappy in China, and this is your excuse to come home and live off of pain pills that you are addicted to!"

It was as though someone had slapped me across the face. I knew it was Satan himself speaking through her. He is no respecter of persons and will speak through anyone to launch his fiery darts. I regained my senses immediately and this time, a righteous anger came on me. She was denying the Miracle Working Power of God. I pointed my finger at her and backed her right into the corner of that little medical room. I said in a bold voice that came up from deep within, "You are out of order, professionally and otherwise." How dare you deny a miracle! Furthermore, I was given 40 pain pills three weeks ago when I left the hospital and I have 39 of them left. God have mercy on you"! I backed away, looking with pity upon her. She took a step towards me and said, "But Joy, you are a Christian, you have to forgive me!"

At that moment I told her she was forgiven, but I would hope in the future, she would be more discreet and have a more compassionate bedside manner towards others, and not deny the power of God when it shows up in a miracle! I reached out and hugged her and assured her that I held no ought against her. I left the office at once and returned to my sister-in-law's home. When I walked in the door, there was a message on the answering machine. It was the doctor. I returned her call at once. She said that her apology was sincere and had hoped there wouldn't be any lawsuits filed on her, or the hospital. I assured her there wouldn't be, and once again all was forgiven.

Debt Cancelled

I had to set up a payment plan with the doctor's office. My doctor's bill was approximately $2,700.00. Two months later, the doctor's office called our office in Broken Arrow and asked our secretary to tell me not to make any more payments as my debt was cancelled. Jesus said, *"This sickness is not unto death but for the glory of God that the Son of God might be glorified thereby"*! Through it all, I had to lean on Jesus. Through it all, I had to take a stand and believe healing belonged to me no matter what it looked like, no matter how bad I felt. Through it all, whenever I pillowed my head on the promises of God at night, I knew my God could not lie. Whatever we go through, if we will just hold fast to what we know, confess the living Word of God and hold the blood of Jesus against every symptom and pain, He will show himself strong and healing will manifest.

There are different avenues to healing. There are different paths to take. As you have seen throughout this book, I have been healed in many different ways. No matter which way, what counts is that we stay with the Word, anchor our souls upon the Word, and let it work for us. Let it have free course in us as our healing Jesus releases the healing balm of Gilead and causes it to flow through our bodies in a miraculous way! Incidentally, the pain in my leg left shortly after the episode that I had in the doctor's office. After returning home, I knelt down before the Lord, and praised him for healing me from the crown of my head to the sole's of my feet. I was pain free within days after that.

CHAPTER 9

CONCLUSION

—+—

The Divine Physician Invites You to Come

At some time or another, no matter who we are, we most likely will need healing in our bodies. We need a visitation from the Divine Physician. He will not visit you unless He is welcomed to do so. So many have closed their hearts to a visitation from the Divine Physician, Jesus. He makes house calls, and personal bedside hospital visits, but He must be called upon first. He will not push or shove or invade. But He will lovingly come at the beckon of every call. He will come and sup with you, and personally nurse you back to health and wholeness! He will prescribe the most powerful medication there is available with no side effects. And even should symptoms get worse, He will tell you double up on the medicine, and guarantee there will be no side effects, neither is it possible to overdose on His medicine.

Every dose of the medication you take will be a new and fresh dose. He will make free deliveries if you will call upon him.

Proverbs 4:20 -22 My son attend to my words, Incline thine ear unto my sayings Let them not depart from my eyes, Keep them in the midst of thine heart. For they are life to those that find them, and health (medicine) to all their flesh.

This medicine, God's Word, is capable and has the power to change your body. Just as you would take a prescribed dose of medication in the natural, you must take your doses of God's medicine properly. Not sporadically, here and there or whenever you feel a pain or a symptom rise. But you must be diligent to take it often. How often? As often as needed! Just as you would rely on natural medicine to heal you, you have to rely on God's Word, His medicine to heal you. Sink yourself into the Word. Let it be your daily diet. His Word will change your body every time you take a fresh dose. This medication never expires! It is fresh, and it is health and life to your body! It is health! You must speak its life giving power over yourself, and you must speak it with faith in your heart. You mind might be telling you one thing, but believe in your heart.

Go to the Lord's table often and commune with Him there. Take faith with you when you go to sup with Him. Bring to your remembrance all that has been provided for you at the cross. Healing has been provided for you. Settle some things at the table. Healing belongs to you, and so claim what is rightfully yours In Jesus Name!

If Satan has visited you or attacked you with a "sickness unto death" go to the communion table many times a day. Set yourself in the Presence of God! Put a praise and worship tape on and sit in His presence. Charge the atmosphere of your home with praise and worship music. Sit alone with God, your loving Father. Call healing into your body!

Faith calls those things that be not as though they were. (Romans 4:17)

Let His Presence be your dwelling place!

Psalm 23:6 I shall dwell in the house of the Lord forever.

In other words He is your dwelling place.

You are a child of God. Go to that secret place, dwell there, live there and abide under the shadow of the Almighty. Go boldly into the Holy of Holies and proclaim and decree that,

by His stripes you are healed! (1Peter 2:24)

Build yourself up and pray in the Spirit. Your inner man needs to be recharged! Praying in the Spirit will quicken your mind and your body. It will refresh your spirit, soul, and body!

Be bold, be strong for the Lord your God is with you!

He is with you! You are not going through this alone! Be bold in His presence. Don't back out, back off, or back down. Rise and be healed in Jesus Name. He's a healing

Jesus who loves to heal. He wants you healed more than you want to be healed!

If you are sick and need a doctor, by all means go to one. But don't go alone. Get the Divine Physician involved in your case. He will give your doctor wisdom beyond his years how to diagnose and treat you, if you will ask for it for him. If you need to take medicine prescribed by a doctor, take it, but once again pray over it with faith, believing for it to be an aid to your healing.

I can't stress this point enough. God loves you and wants you well. He gets no pleasure in seeing his child or children sick. He wants you well, and he wants you to press toward the mark for the prize of the high calling of God in Christ Jesus! He takes pleasure in seeing you prosper and be in health even as your soul prospers. He takes pleasure in the prosperity of his children. When you are prospering, and that is by means of being healthy, God is pleased. It delights HIM to see us walking in health.

We must be aware that the devil will want to make every effort to launch an attack on you. Sickness comes from the devil. He wants to bring weakness and infirmity to your spirit, soul, and body. Resist him, give him no place, and refuse to give in. Rise up and be determined to overcome with a strong spirit. Do not give up any ground. Be strong and exercise your authority as the Word directs you to do, and you will gain the victory.

Luke 10:19 Behold, I give you power to tread on serpents and scorpions, and over all the power of the enemy; and nothing shall by any means hurt you.

I trust the writing of this book have been an encouragement to all who are sick and suffering with disease in their bodies. May God be glorified as you accept His Word as medicine to your flesh, and you too can then say what Jesus said when a bad report was given. You can then believe the report of the Lord, stand in faith for your healing to manifest, and bring Glory to our Master, our Lord and Savior, Jesus Christ.

Prayer

—+—

All through the Bible prayer has forever been life changing and powerful. The same power you read about throughout the scriptures from Genesis to Revelations is available to you right now. When God himself is involved in the prayer prayed over the situation, the circumstance, the sickness and disease, his anointing power is always present to heal. The book of James says that prayer can heal and restore people. *(James 5:6)*

Praying For You:

Father I come to you in the Name of Jesus. I pray for all those who are standing on your Word for their healing to manifest in their bodies. I pray for the joy of the Lord to be their strength, as they would be neither grieved or oppressed, but that they would be strong in you and in the power of your might. May they press on, stand strong, and never give up. You are greater than any sickness and disease. I take authority over sickness and disease that has launched an attack on their bodies, and I command it to leave. Tumors dry up and be gone, hearts beat with the rhythm of life, blood pressures be normal, organs be whole, brains be quick, smart, sharp and alert with divine supernatural instant memory recall. All joints, muscles, nerves and tendons be whole. Every disorder I command you to come into order. I loose the burden removing, yoke destroying anointing of God to flow and break every yoke of sickness and disease in every body. I thank you for the release of the healing balm of Gilead as it flows from the crown of their heads to the very souls of their feet. We thank you for quick recoveries, healed and whole bodies, in Jesus Name.

Healing Scriptures
for Meditation

—+—

*P*roverbs 4:20 -22 My son attend to my words; incline thine ear unto my sayings. Let them not depart from thine eyes; keep them in the midst of thine heart. For they are life unto those that find them and health (or medicine) to all their flesh.

Romans 4:19-21 And being not weak in faith, he considered not his own body now dead, when he was about an hundred years old, neither yet the deadness of Sarah's womb. He staggered not at the promise of God through unbelief; but was strong in faith, giving glory to God.

Luke 5:17 And the power of the Lord was present to heal them.

Mark 5:28 For she said, If I may touch but his clothes, I shall be whole.

Romans 10:17 So then faith cometh by hearing and hearing by the word of God.

Hebrews 12:2 Looking unto Jesus the author and finisher of our faith; who for the joy that was set before him endured the cross, despising the shame, and is set down at the right hand of the throne of God.

Matthew 8:17 That it might be fulfilled which was spoken by Esaias the prophet, saying, HIMSELF TOOK OUR INFIRMITIES, AND BARE OUR SICKNESS.

Isaiah 53:1 Who hath believed our report? And to whom is the arm of the Lord revealed?

Isaiah 53:4-5 Surely he hath borne our griefs, and carried our sorrows: Yet we did esteem him stricken, smitten of God, and afflicted. But he was wounded for our transgressions, he was bruised for our iniquities: the chastisement of our peace was upon him; and with his stripes we are healed.

Psalm 107:20 He sent his word and healed them, and delivered them from their destruction.

Psalm 103:3 Who forgiveth all thine iniquities; who healeth all thy diseases.

1Peter 2:24 Who his own self bare our sins in his own body on the tree, that we being dead to sins, should live unto righteousness by whose stripes ye were healed.

James 1:17 Every good and every perfect gift is from above, and cometh down from the Father of lights, with whom is no variableness, neither shadow of turning.

John 5:13-15 Is any among you afflicted? Let him pray. Is any merry? Let him sing songs. Is any sick among you? Let him call for the elders of the church; and let them pray over him, anointing him with oil in the name of the Lord: And the prayer of faith shall save the sick, and the Lord shall raise him up; and if he has committed sins they shall be forgiven him.

Salvation Invitation

—+—

If you do not know Jesus Christ, and have never had an opportunity to receive him into your heart, and make him Lord of your life, today can be your day to allow him to be your Lord and Savior. God loves you, and cares about every aspect of your life. That is why he sent his only begotten son to die for you. I encourage you to make your life right with God, and make heaven your eternal home this very moment.

According to

Romans 10: 9-10 That if thou shalt confess with thy mouth the Lord Jesus and shalt believe in thine heart that God hath raised him from the dead, thou shalt be saved. For with the heart man believeth unto righteousness; and with the mouth confession is made unto salvation.

Please pray this prayer out loud now:

God, I repent of my sins, and ask you to forgive me of all wrong doing. I believe You sent Jesus to die on the cross for me. I now believe in God the Father, the

Son, and the Holy Spirit. I receive Jesus Christ as my own personal Lord and Savior. I now confess Him as Lord of my life and I give my entire life to Him. I am now born anew, a new creation in Christ Jesus. Thank you for saving me. Amen.

If you have prayed this prayer, welcome to the family of God.

Prayer Notes

———+———

U se this space to jot down thoughts that the Holy reading this book. Use it also as a mini prayer journal. Use it to record favorite scriptures, and healing testimonies that you receive from God.

About the Author

———+———

Joy Haynes is a international speaker, author and missionary to China. She is a graduate of Rhema Bible Training Center in Broken Arrow, Oklahoma. It was there that she met her husband Rick and they were soon married. After graduating from Rhema in 1995, they moved to China in August and have lived there for 11 years now as missionary's. Joy and Rick founded China Harvest Ministries in May 1995 and opened a branch office in Dalian, China in 2000.

They have taught both underground and legal pastors and leaders in China. In 1996 they were arrested for teaching a group of Chinese leaders and God miraculously set them free just like Paul and Silas in Acts 16. In 1994, Joy and her husband smuggled seven suitcases of Bibles from Hong Kong to Shanghai to an 81 year old woman.

They started an orphanage in 2000 in a village just outside of Dalian. Joy has managed that orphanage with 16 children for 7 years now. You can see the orphanage at www. chinaharvest.org

Joy has been ministering God's Word to the lost and hurting since 1993. She is especially used by God to minister healing to the sick. She is available for Healing Meetings in your church.

<u>If you would like for Joy to come and speak at your church then please contact us.</u>

Contact:
Joy Haynes
China Harvest Ministries
PO Box 2074
Broken Arrow, OK 74013
918-438-4464
www.chinaharvest.org

Printed in the United States
84490LV00004B/178-426/A